Exploring tough questions facing youth today

THE RADICAL REIGN

Parables of Jesus

ISBN 978-1-949628-18-0
Printed in the United States of America.
10 9 8 7 6 5 4 3 2 1   22 21 20 19

Published by The Pastoral Center, http://pastoral.center.

Developed in partnership with MennoMedia and Brethren Press. Series editors: Fumiaki Tosu, Ann Naffziger, and Paul Canavese. *The Radical Reign:* Writer, Gary Wilde. Project editor, Lani Wright. Staff editors, Susan E. Janzen, Julie Garber, and James Deaton. Updated design, Paul Stocksdale.

All rights reserved. Purchase of this book includes a license to reproduce this resource for use in a single parish, school, or other similar organization. You are allowed to share and make unlimited copies only for use within the organization that licensed it. If you serve more than one organization, each should purchase its own license. You may not post this document to any web site without explicit permission to do so. Outside of these conditions, no part of this book may be reproduced in any form or by any means, electronic or mechanical, including photocopying, recording, taping, or via any retrieval system, without the written permission of The Pastoral Center, 1212 Versailles Ave., Alameda, CA 94501. Thank you for cooperating with our honor system regarding our licenses.

For questions or to order additional copies or licenses, please call 1-844-727-8672 or visit http://pastoral.center.

Portions of this work © 2019 by The Pastoral Center / PastoralCenter.com. Adapted and published with permission from Generation Why Bible Studies. © 1995, 2014 Brethren Press, Elgin, IL 60120 and MennoMedia, Harrisonburg, VA 22803, U.S.A. All rights reserved.

Unless otherwise noted, the Scripture passages contained herein are from the *New Revised Standard Version of the Bible*, copyright © 1989 by the National Council of the Churches of Christ in the United States of America. Used by permission. All rights reserved.

Bible-based Explorations of Issues Facing Youth

» OVERVIEW

When conversing online, the acronym IRL stands for "in real life." The virtual world of social media, text chats, blogs, and more have the power to remove us from the real world. What we experience online can skew our perspective on what it means to be human. It can numb us, incite us, distract us, depress us, confuse us, and make us rude or impatient. Strangely, this supposedly "social" and "connected" technology can profoundly disconnect us from others.

Religious faith can also place us in a bubble, especially when it distances us from others. When we keep the prophetic message at a safe distance, obscured in theological language and abstractions, we are missing the whole point. And when we see our parish as an insider club that serves itself, we can forget the radically inclusive message entrusted to us: God's love is for *everyone*, and God expects us to transform the *whole world* through that love.

Through the incarnation, God showed up in the real world to show us that our faith is not just about talking the talk, but also walking the walk. It can be risky. It can be confusing. It can hurt. But living out our faith can also bring us great purpose, peace, and joy.

This series connects the Bible with the tough questions that youth (and adults) encounter in their neighborhood, in school, among friends, and even online. This process will help you as a leader break open these issues in a fun and meaningful way, sparking conversation and the kind of life change Jesus invites us to embrace.

» THE ROLE OF PARENTS

As children enter middle school and high school, they become more independent, self-reliant, and, well, self-centered. This can bring parents to make assumptions that this is the time to step back, giving their child more space to form their identity. While there is truth to that at some level (adolescents definitely shouldn't be smothered), this is a stage of life when parents should in fact *lean in*. The apparent confidence and bluster youth show on the outside can mask the insecurity and confusion on the inside. Youth need their parents to be involved more than ever.

» WHOLE FAMILY FORMATION

Parents are the primary teachers of their own children, and parishes are waking up to the fact that faith formation programs need to bring parents into the process if they hope to see faith passed on to the next generation. Recent studies give us more and more evidence that the role of parents is the most important factor in determining whether a child will embrace faith as they move toward adulthood. Research from the Center for the Applied Research on the Apostolate shows that parents who talk about their faith and show through their actions that their faith is important to them are more likely to have children who remain Catholic.

More about Whole Family Formation >>>>

To learn more about how your parish can take a comprehensive whole family approach to faith formation, visit **GrowingUpCatholic.com**.

While whole family events with elementary-aged children are on the rise, the role of parents can be an afterthought in youth ministry. We have designed the sessions in this series to work with or without parents present, and we encourage you to offer them as parent-child events.

If you choose to involve parents, it is important to consider before each session how to best do so. Many of the activities in this series are high-energy, creative, or silly. Some parents may need some encouragement to get out of their heads and have fun with the group. A few activities involving physical contact would be inappropriate for parents and youth to participate together, and we have noted them as such.

There are a number of ways to approach discussions with parent participation. Unless you have a small group, you will likely want to break into smaller groups for conversation. Some youth may be self-conscious and unable to be completely honest and open in a group situation with a parent present. For this reason, you may choose in some cases to assign parents to different groups from their own children, or to have separate parent and child groups altogether. Be sure to cover expectations around confidentiality. It is inappropriate for a parent (or youth) to share with another parent what their child said in a small group.

Note that even if parents and their children do not share all conversations together in the session, they will still have a valuable shared experience and can have extended conversations about it later.

>> THANK YOU

The role you play in gathering, animating, praying with, and forming youth is a valuable one. Thank you for all you do to serve the church and its families!

Bible-based Explorations of Issues Facing Youth

THE RADICAL REIGN
Parables of Jesus

>> INTRODUCTION

Parables are "I" openers. First they get our attention with their controversial, "against the grain" style and message. Then they open up our spiritual "eyes" and reveal, with startling clarity, the nature of God and the reign of Heaven. Perhaps the most amazing thing about the parables is that they have the power to either strengthen faith and move us closer to reign-of-God ideals, OR they can harden us in our unbelief. In either case, Jesus' parables always call for personal decision, related to every area of our life with God.

Jesus turned people's worlds upside down when he told them—through parables—what God is really like. He revealed God's reign as radically different from the world we live in. What's so different about it?

First, **God's love is unconditional**. Even though grace may be a good idea, some people may wish God would give it out sparingly, and to those who earn it. Yet the parable of the vineyard workers and the parables of the lost sheep and the lost coin teach that no one has more access to God than another, and people can do nothing to earn that love.

Second, **the call to live in the radical reign is being sounded NOW**. In the parable of the great feast, Jesus confronted the human tendency to ignore a gracious invitation from God. We find other needs and desires to be more pressing. Yet the moment of decision for the reign of God keeps confronting us.

Third, **we can't go it alone**. Against the backdrop of the North American worship of rugged individualism, we find instead that our true source of life comes from being connected—to the Vine and to the other branches.

Fourth, **the gospel is essentially the subversion of the usual order**. Jesus' parables not only talked about the radical reign of God, they called for action, a radical way of living. Through the parables of the Pharisee and the tax collector and the good Samaritan, Jesus called us to upend our traditional perspective, because "the last will be first and the first last."

The people who heard Jesus speak so long ago were hardly different from us in their need for a vibrant spiritual life. Some drank up his words with thirsty souls, and longed for more. Others were turned off by his radical statements about God's way of loving and judging. How will it be with you and your group? Let those who have eyes truly see!

>>>
"Through its concreteness the language of Jesus captures our attention, through its rhythmic cadences it resonates in our memories, and through its puzzles and enigmas it engages our quest for understanding."

John R. Donahue, S.J.,
The Gospel in Parable

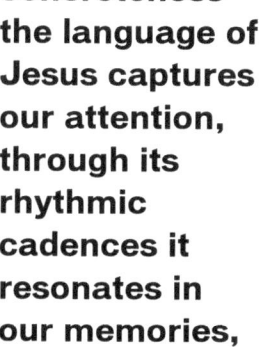

EXTENDER SESSION

Most units include one extender session, with suggestions for special activities related to the issue of the unit. Extender sessions help accommodate the diversity of parish schedules. Since each unit is undated, youth may study units in their entirely and still participate in special events of the parish that get scheduled simultaneously with youth group time. Extender sessions can be used anytime, but the one for this unit best follows **Session 4.** Calculate now whether or not you will be using the extender session.

THE TEACHING PLAN: The parts of the session guide

>> **Faith story.** The session is rooted in this Bible passage.

>> **Faith focus.** This is the story of the passage in a nutshell.

>> **Session goal.** The entire session is built around this goal. What changes—in knowledge, attitude, and/or action—do you desire in your group?

>> **Materials needed and advance preparation.** This is what you will need if the session is to go smoothly. You'll feel more at ease if you've taken care of these details before you meet your group.

>> FROM LIFE TO BIBLE TO LIFE

The teaching plan we use is called *life-centered*. However, when we write each session, we always begin with Scripture. We ask, what does this particular passage say, especially to youth? Each teaching session moves from life to Bible to life. So the Bible is really at the center of this way of teaching.

In every session we try to hit upon a tough question that participants might ask. Find out what questions on this issue are important for your group. Feel free to bring your own input and invite your group members to add their own experiences.

>> TEACHING THE SESSION

The five step-by-step movements will carry you from *life to the Bible and back to life*. Each session takes about 45 to 50 minutes. If there is a handout sheet for the session, take note of any complementary activities and stories.

1. **Focus.** This activity is intended to create a friendly climate within the group and to draw attention to the issue.

2. **Connect.** Talking, drawing, role playing, and other activities invite participants to express their own life experience about the issue. Also use memory, reason, or imagination to get the group thinking about *why* they view the issue the way they do.

3. **Explore the Bible.** With a minimum of lecturing, dig into the faith story and search for answers to questions raised in the first activities. The Insights from Scripture section will help clarify the faith story. Help participants discover how the faith community understands the Bible passage.

4. **Apply** the faith story. This is the "aha!" moment when participants realize the faith story has wisdom for *their* lives.

5. **Respond.** What will the group do about the issue in light of what they have learned from their own experiences set alongside the faith story? At this point, the faith story becomes lived rather than a mere intellectual exercise.

>> LOOK AHEAD

Here are reminders for what you need to do for the next session or two.

>> INSIGHTS FROM SCRIPTURE

Here is a resource for Explore the Bible. Don't try to use all the material given. Take what you need to lead the session and answer questions your group may have. Let the Insights section inspire you to think and study more about the Bible passage for the session.

›› HANDOUT SHEETS

Occasionally, there will be a handout sheet to complement your session. If you choose to use this, you will need to make enough copies for the group. These sheets may include questions, stories, agree/disagree exercises, charts, pictures, and other materials to stimulate your group to think and discuss.

Generally, no participant preparation is required unless the session plan calls for you to contact selected group members for specific tasks.

>>> SESSION 1

NO FAIR! >>>

>> KEY VERSE

"These last worked only one hour, and you have made them equal to us who have borne the burden of the day and the scorching heat." (Matthew 20:12)

>> FAITH STORY

Matthew 19:27–20:15 (The parable of the vineyard workers)

>> FAITH FOCUS

Just after Jesus told a rich young man to sell his possessions in order to have treasure in heaven, Peter asked, "What's in it for us, who *do* leave everything to follow?" Jesus responded with the **parable of the vineyard workers**.

In our relationship with God, our acceptance is not based on how hard we work. It is based purely on God's desire to show us divine love. No one has more access to the love of God than another, and people can do nothing to earn that love. For youth, who are competing on many fronts, this parable can be an important insight into the unconditional quality of God's love.

>> SESSION GOAL

As participants approach their lives with a "get the best bang for the buck" mentality, help them confront the parable's radical message of God's unconditional love.

>> **Materials needed and advance preparation**

- Chalkboard/chalk or newsprint/markers
- Paper and pencils
- Prepare sign-up sheets (see Focus, Option A)
- Construction paper and crayons (see Respond)
- Mini-candy bars or mini-cookies (see Respond, Option B)

TEACHING PLAN

1. FOCUS 7-8 minutes

>> **Option A** (for indoor setting):
Ask participants to imagine that the church board has given them the task of remodeling (or decorating) their meeting room—for pay! The whole group receives $1,000. Give the group 3-4 minutes to generate a list about what tasks they'd want to have done (paint, rearrange furniture, new floor, etc.). Then pass around sign-up sheets for getting the work done. Divide the sign-up sheets in half lengthwise, and put headings at the top:

GIRLS
(receive $30 for every hour worked)

GUYS
(receive $30 for every 4 hours worked)

In Real Life | The Radical Reign

Have the girls sign up on one side, and the guys on the other. When someone complains about the unfairness of the wages, let them grumble a bit, then point out that everyone should be thankful for getting paid at all for decorating their room! Then move right into the discussion on fairness in Connect.

>> **Option B** (for camp/retreat setting):

Choose one or more of the following tasks (or come up with one of your own) as a contest:

- *whoever swims the most miles*
- *whoever walks/hikes the most miles*
- *whoever reads the most Bible verses*

Announce that you will be awarding a prize (monetary, honorary, culinary) to the person who wins the contest. Make a big deal of the task/contest. This could even be over a period of days, all leading up to this session. When you give out the prize, however, award it first to the person who won the contest, then **give the same prize** to everyone else in the group. Use this to generate a discussion about fairness. How do the people who *didn't* win the contest feel? How does the person who won the contest feel?

2. CONNECT 5-8 minutes

Ask participants about times when they have felt taken advantage of in the area of "workload." For instance, have they ever felt they got paid less than another person did for an equal amount of work? Can they recall times when they were asked to do work that others didn't have to do? How did they feel about that? In other words: *When did you most feel, "Hey! No fair! I'm having to do all this, and they don't have to do* **anything**!" Likely such situations have occurred among siblings. Invite people to tell their stories. Then follow up with these questions: *Is it possible to make sure that life is always fair? Suppose life really were strictly fair and just—everybody always got exactly what they deserved. What would that kind of world look like? Would anything be missing?*

Shift to the next activity by saying: *We all want things to be fair in this life. but even if we could guarantee perfect fairness and get exactly what we deserve, we'd be missing something—the opportunity to be given something we DON'T deserve! Let's find out more....*

3. EXPLORE THE BIBLE 10-12 minutes

Choose a way to designate the categories FAIR and NO FAIR! at opposite sides of the room. Then prepare participants to hear Matthew 19:27–20:15 by giving them a listening assignment. As you read, they are to make a mental note of *at least one thing in the passage that they would describe as either FAIR or NO FAIR*. After the reading they should move to one end of the room and be ready to tell about their FAIR/NO FAIR reaction.

Now read aloud the Bible passage. After participants move to the ends of the room, ask:

- *What did you think was FAIR? NO FAIR?*
- *What was the point of Jesus' story?* (Possible answers: everyone is equal before God; all kinds of work are essentially the same in God's eyes; divine generosity is available to all who look for it)
- *What either* encourages *you or* bothers *you about this "point"?*
- *Is God fair or unfair in this story? Tell why you think so. Are there other words to describe how God acts in this parable, besides fair and unfair?* (Possible answers: merciful, graceful, generous)

Draw on the material in Insights from Scripture to summarize the basic message of the parable. Say something like: *God is generous in ways that may strike us as "unfair"—one-hour workers getting a full day's pay! However, in our relationship with God, our acceptance is not based on how hard we work. It is based purely on God's desire to show us divine love. Actually, we can be thankful that strict justice doesn't prevail!*

If you have time, follow up with one more discussion question: *Why should we be "good workers," if just about anyone will get the same "pay"?*

4. APPLY 15 minutes

>>> **Option A:** Tell the group to think about raising money to go to a youth gathering. Have them work together to decide what they would do to raise money.

Then—as individuals, pairs, or small groups—participants should decide these three things (write them on the board):

- What tasks they would want done
- How they would divide up the responsibilities fairly (exactly equally, considering differences in strength, ability, etc.)
- How they would divide the money (i.e., who gets how much, and when?)

Circulate among the participants to answer questions and give further guidance as they work. When everyone has come up with some ideas, ask: *WHY do you feel your plan would be a fair way to accomplish this work? What things could happen that might make it unfair?* (For example: Some kids might not show up to work; others might goof off. Or some might be underpaid, even though they put in extra effort.) *Since this work is for a special youth gathering, would it matter to you if the money distribution was fair or unfair? Why or why not?*

>>> **Option B:** If you have a sports-oriented group, enact a "generic" sports contract case. Any sports fan will quickly recognize the constant battle between sports superstars and their team owners to renegotiate their contracts as rookies come into the league. Divide into two "teams," **players** and **owners**. Then bring up a recent case in point, with real names, if possible, which will very likely go like this:

> *I.B.J. Superstar signed a contract three years ago for 7 million dollars over the next five years. He was very happy for the first two years of the contract. Now, however, management has signed Mr. Awesome Rookie, right out of college, for a contract of 10 million dollars over four years.*

Give the "players" team up to 30 seconds to respond to the "owners." (Mr. Superstar might say some-thing like: "I've had a great two years. But Rookie hasn't even played in the league yet! Why am I getting paid less? I want a new contract.")

Then give the "owners" up to 30 seconds to respond. (This might go something like: "Hey, you liked the contract when you signed it. It was fair and generous. And a contract is a contract, so abide by it and like it. What we do with other players is none of your business.")

Then discuss: *How is this sports contract conflict like, and unlike, what happens in Jesus' parable?*

LOOK AHEAD

For the next session, develop a list of injuries that might come into an emergency room. In advance, contact a nurse or doctor in your congregation and ask them to arrange your list in a triage order (see the triage explanation in Session 2). Also, make homemade transfer ink (Respond, *Option B*).

5. RESPOND 5-10 minutes

 Option A: Make "Grace in My Life" statements. Hand each person a piece of construction paper, and make crayons or markers available. Invite everyone to make an artistic acrostic (ready to decorate the walls) with the three initials of their first, middle, and last names. Stipulate that the statements must be about things in their life, or about them, that indicate the workings of God's grace. For example:

G = God's child
A = Always forgiven
W = Wonderful friends

Hang the Grace Acrostics on the walls and offer a closing prayer.

 Option B: For a snack, tell people you are going to hand out mini-candy bars (or, for a larger group, use mini-cookies). Let participants watch you take out a grocery bag and count out (loudly and carefully) the same amount of bars or cookies as the number of group members. Lay the pieces out on a table, and then say: "Starting with (*name of a participant*), come get your snack."

When "Sue" takes only one of the pieces (because you've counted out the same number as the number of people in the group), let her know that her portion *is the whole amount placed on the table*. Then, one at a time, give everyone else *that same number of pieces*.

Close by offering a prayer of thanks for God's surprising grace!

> "The parable speaks of how this new reality [of God's boundless generosity] is breaking into the weariness and hopelessness of the people of God. It is an outrageous process. It makes the lowest into the hightest; it awakens deep anxieties; it causes scandal. But it also allows hope to bloom and bestows deep joy."
>
> Gerhard Lohfink
> *Jesus of Nazareth*

 # INSIGHTS FROM SCRIPTURE

Just after Jesus spoke to the rich young man (in Matt. 19:16-26), Peter piped up, "We have left everything and followed you! What then will we have?" If giving up earthly riches was the requirement, then surely the disciples easily qualified for the maximum reward.

So Jesus told his disciples a story, using commonplace props, to help them see that God's favor cannot be earned. In the parable of the vineyard workers (found only in Matthew), God's love is given freely and unconditionally to all who present themselves.

>> THE ECCENTRIC FARMER

In the Middle East, grapes normally ripened at the end of September and the rains came soon after—heavy rains that could devastate the entire crop. It was a race to get the harvest in. The vineyard owner went to the labor pool at 6 a.m. (sunrise, or the first hour, in the Jewish way of reckoning). He went again at 9 a.m., noon, 3 p.m., and 5 p.m., looking for anyone willing to work, for any length of time.

When it came time to disperse the pay, the last paid naturally expected more, since they had seen the other workers receiving a full day's wage. Yet—surprise!—the owner's heart was apparently touched. Or maybe he was "touched in the head." Obviously, one hour's worth of pay wouldn't feed a worker's family, and the owner proved to be generous to those who worked a partial day, even as little as an hour.

>> IDENTIFYING THE CONNECTIONS

Though a parable typically makes only one main point, we can make certain figurative connections in this way:

- **Hours** = measures of accomplishment
- **Field** = Heaven
- **Landowner** = metaphor for God
- **Marketplace** = labor pool (the lowest class of workers, whose daily lives were more precarious than even slaves, who at least had some connection to a family)

The most intriguing question of identity is, of course, *Who are the workers?* Bible scholars raise at least three possible interpretations:

1. The groups represent a progression of generations in God's salvation history, with Christians or Gentiles symbolized as the eleventh-hour workers.
2. The different worker groups signify the different stages of life when people come to belief.
3. The workers are a symbol of the development of the Christian church. The older churches are the early morning workers and younger churches are the later arrivals.

As interesting as it may be to speculate on such symbols, it is vastly more important to grasp the point Jesus was making about the nature of God.

>> WHAT IS GOD LIKE?

God is not "fair." Regardless of whether you and your group identify with the "early" workers or the "late" workers, this parable hits hard. Issues of "fairness" can wrench our stomachs. It's hard to swallow the idea that God could give equal pay for unequal labor. It's the same issue the elder brother had to deal with in the story of the prodigal son (Luke 15:11-32)—"Why should I work my tail off and never get offered a party, when my no-account brother, who only lately showed any family loyalty, gets the fatted calf?"

But neither the boys' father nor the vineyard owner was a stingy tyrant abusing his workers. The issue of fairness in these cases was that both the father and the owner were being *too* fair. What a wake-up call to the older brother! What a twist on an old labor-versus-owners story! And how did the father respond? "You've always had access to me and to my wealth. Why do you begrudge your brother my love?" People believe God gives out grace, but perhaps they'd like to see God give it out sparingly, "fairly," and according to their own ideas of deserving.

>> DIVINE GENEROSITY

Is the point then that everyone is equal before God? Or that all kinds of work for God are essentially the same? Perhaps. But it seems better to focus on something even more basic: God goes beyond the normal conventions of fairness—divine generosity is available to all who look for it. This may indeed strike us as radical, perhaps even "unfair." But could we survive if it were any other way? For all of us have "become like one who is unclean, and all our righteous deeds are like a filthy cloth" (Is. 64:6) and "all have sinned and fall short of the glory of God" (Rom. 3:23). Thank God that divine love is radically generous. Those who give their whole lives to God receive divine generosity and companionship all that time. And those who come later are invited in with the same promises and love.

SESSION 2

THE GREAT FEAST

KEY VERSES

"At the time for the dinner he sent his slave to say to those who had been invited, 'Come, for everything is ready now.' But they all alike began to make excuses." (Luke 14:17-18a)

FAITH STORY

Luke 14:15-24 (The parable of the great feast)

FAITH FOCUS

In the **parable of the great feast**, Jesus confronted the human tendency to ignore a gracious invitation from God. We find other needs and desires to be more pressing. We make excuses and go our way. Yet the moment of decision for the Way of love keeps confronting us: Will we throw our lot in with Jesus, or will we be drawn off by the temptations of the world? The call to this dinner speaks primarily to our freedom to either hold on to, or let go of, what we have planned for our own salvation.

SESSION GOAL

Challenge participants to arrange their daily tasks with a new awareness of the importance of God's radical reign.

TEACHING PLAN

Materials needed and advance preparation

- Pencils
- Index cards
- Chalkboard/chalk or newsprint/markers
- Bibles
- Copies of handout sheet for Session 2
- List of injuries that might come into an emergency room (see Focus, *Option A* for suggestions). Ask a nurse or doctor in your congregation to arrange your list in a triage order (who would receive treatment first, second, third, etc.), then jot the injuries on index cards, one per card.
- Medical equipment (*optional*)
- Homemade transfer ink, watercolor brush, card stock or plain notecards, pictures for "printing" (see Respond, *Option B*)

1. FOCUS 10-15 minutes minutes

In advance, come up with a list of injuries that might come into an emergency room (make some of them humorous or ridiculous). For example: broken leg, thumb cut off, stung by 200 killer bees, overdosed on Mango Cocktail Snapple, unconscious from carbon monoxide poisoning, hangnail on big toe, etc. Then ask a nurse or doctor in your church to arrange your list in a triage order, based on who should receive treatment first, second, third, etc. Finally, jot the injuries on index cards, one per card, and bring the cards to your meeting. Also, in the center of the room, make available any medical equipment you can gather, for instance: bandages, slings, crutches, thermometers, aspirin bottles (but just bandages and gauze would be sufficient).

Open the session by explaining the concept of triage: "allocating treatment according to a system of priorities designed to maximize the number of survivors" (Webster). Then say: *Imagine! You're all injured in a strange coincidence of accidents and disasters. You all arrive at* the emergency room at once! Your task is to arrange yourself in a line, by priority of injury: who should receive treatment first, second, third, etc. Then give them instructions in this order:

1. Here's an injury card for each person (hand out cards). Keep it secret for now.
2. You'll have 5 minutes to find a partner and guess each other's injuries. You can answer questions only with YES or NO.
3. Once you've guessed the injury, use the medical supplies to "dress" your partner's wound.
4. Finally, work with the whole group to form a triage line. See whether you can come up with the same triage order a nurse or doctor suggested.

Say "GO!" and let pandemonium reign for a few minutes as participants guess one another's injuries, bandage one another, and finally arrange themselves in an order they think would correspond with a
doctor's decisions. Then "judge" the decisions by showing everyone the professional triage decisions.

"The Gospel of Luke intends to point Christian communities to a radical interpretation of the Torah and the rights it gives to the poor… [H]unger among the people requires the opening of the houses of those who have enough to eat… The experience of sharing food – and economic resources – with the poor evokes… happiness, just as does the nearness of God that is celebrated in these meals."

Luise Schottroff,
The Parables of Jesus

2. CONNECT 7-8 minutes
Follow up the triage activity with some discussion about prioritizing. Ask:

- How did you decide whose injuries first needed treatment?
- How do you "triage" your daily life's activities and responsibilities? What gets first priority? Second? Third?
- What decisions do you make every day that help you "survive" the tug and pull of everything you could be doing?
- What <u>major decisions</u> have you had to make in your life so far? Did any have serious consequences (perhaps even life-and-death results)? What were the options you faced? <u>WHY</u> did you choose a particular course of action in that situation?
- Think (in silence): Where does God (or the church) fit into all of this decision making?

Shift to the next activity by saying: *It's a real challenge to recognize and choose what's most important in our lives. We have so many options, how do we make sure we don't miss something that may have eternal significance? Jesus told a parable about that dilemma.*

3. EXPLORE THE BIBLE 5-8 minutes
Ask: *Have you ever been invited to an event, turned it down because you had other things to do, and then found out later that it was great? What happened?*

Assign parts for the three excuse-makers, and read Luke 14:15-24 together. Then ask for reactions to the parable, as if participants were sitting around the table when Jesus actually spoke the words. After some discussion, briefly supplement their ideas with additional information, drawing on material from Insights from Scripture. Follow up by asking:

- Would you agree or disagree with someone who says: "Religion is always less exciting than real life"? What would those in the parable have said?
- If you were someone in the parable, who would you be? (An excuse-maker? the person in verse 15? the host? Or, make up your own part and explain it….)

4. APPLY 10-12 minutes

Distribute pencils and the handout sheet, "Time to Eat...Come on In!" Ask: *Suppose a friend were to walk up to you and say: "Look, you can't see God, and the Reign of love is a joke! Focus on reality, not pie-in-the-sky! Get on with your life and let the religious people take care of church things. Don't sweat it!"*

Field some responses, and then go over the instructions on the handout sheet. Allow a few minutes for people to fill in their sheets (or just jot some notes) before sharing some of their responses. (Have some fun with the "kid-age memory" section by asking teens to be specific about the kinds of play they found exciting when they were little.) Follow up with one or more of these questions:

- *Do you ever offer excuses to God? If so, how are your excuses like, or unlike, the excuses in the parable of the great feast?*
- *Why do you think God gives us the freedom to decline a gracious invitation? Who has the responsibility for the consequences when that happens?*
- *What could our church do to help proclaim God's banquet invitation in a more real and relevant way to people today? On the other hand, what might be a way for a young person to "solve" his or her excuse problem?*

5. RESPOND 8-10 minutes

>> **Option A:** First do a quote-reaction exercise to launch the closing activity. Write this quotation on the chalkboard or newsprint:

"The urgent is never important; the important is never urgent."

Ask: *Do you agree or disagree with this statement? If the people in the parable had really believed this, how might it have changed their responses?*

Wrap up the session by inviting everyone to do a quick "triage" of their daily activities. Hand out four index cards to each person and ask them to put one of their responsibilities, decisions, opportunities, or relationships on each card. They are to arrange the cards in order of priority. Have them think about how much importance these items have for them; how much thought, influence, time and energy these things require.

If the group seems willing, ask them to join their original partners from the opening activity and to share with one another about their daily activity triages. Invite them to offer a prayer for each other about any of the items to which *they would like to give greater or less priority* in their lives.

>> **Option B:** (for youth group or retreat setting):

As a way of proclaiming God's banquet invitation, make your own "act NOW," "seize the day," or "*carpe diem*" messages on notecards or event T-shirts and bandanas. Choose designs or pictures that catch the spirit of the parable of the great feast—from funny papers or newspaper ads (any printed matter works, though slick paper doesn't work as well). Choose designs that look as good "backward" as they do "forward," since you'll print a mirror image. Then transfer the designs to the cards or cloth using homemade transfer ink:

Dissolve 2 tablespoons **scrapings from a bar of soap** in ¼ cup **hot water**. Add 1 tablespoon **turpentine**. When cool, pour into a screw-top bottle. To use the ink, brush it over the picture to be transferred with a **watercolor brush**. Place a piece of paper (heavier paper or card stock works well) or fabric over the picture and rub the back of it with a spoon. Transfer ink can be stored indefinitely without refrigeration.

>>>
LOOK AHEAD

For activities in the next session, you'll need at least 100 pennies and a paper bill (see details in Session 3). As an option, show a brief scene from the movie *Ferris Bueller's Day Off*. Cue up to the right spot, ready to show. (Preview the scene to be sure it is appropriate for your group. Some of the words may be considered offensive.)

"God brings into our lives the loss of what we have been holding on to, what identifies us, what is 'saving' our ego. We are forced to let it go and given the opportunity to just BE in [God's] love."

Gerald May,
The Awakened Heart

 # INSIGHTS FROM SCRIPTURE

The parable of the great feast, like the one about the vineyard laborers, is directed primarily to Jesus' critics and opponents in order to show that the good news of God's radical reign overcomes their legalistic approach to life. This good news is spurned by the very ones so graciously invited to hear and accept it. Why? Because "more important" matters concerned those potential banqueters. The parable, then, is a story of the excuses we humans make when our attention becomes riveted to earthly concerns, dulling our sensitivity to the immediacy, reality, and goodness of God's reign.

WORLD OF EXCUSES

This banquet invitation went to well-meaning, well-mannered, and wealthy people. They were invited first because they had the most to be thankful for—they were the ones who ought to have been celebrating. But there were no RSVPs. The host *expected* their attendance. So when the dinner was ready, all made excuses! All said no! The first two based their excuses on simple materialism. Our possessions can certainly get in the way of our commitment to God's reign of God. It was true in Jesus' day, and it is perhaps even more of a problem today, seeing how much more "material" there is to divert our attention.

The third person raised a potentially valid excuse in the ancient Hebrew society. The scriptures said: "When a man is newly married, he shall not go out with the army or be charged with any related duty. He shall be free at home one year, to be happy with the wife whom he has married" (Deut. 24:5). Yet, could this invitation really be considered a duty? Just as a gracious host may be turned down, so God's gracious offer of salvation may be snubbed.

WORD FROM GOD

How shall we interpret this parable? On one level it is simply a story about the danger of presumption. The invited guests needed reminding that the blessedness of partaking in God's reign comes only to those who are willing wholeheartedly to accept the invitation when it comes. This may not be convenient, especially if we are caught up in gratifying our own self-interest rather than following God's loving way.

On a broader level, scholars have placed the parable in the context of other stories Jesus told, stories that warned the Jews that God's saving invitation only *starts* with them, and extends to all people. As Bible commentator D. A. Carson puts it:

> "Although Jesus does not interpret the parable, it is reasonable to link it with 13:28-30 and find in it an allusion of the extension of the gospel to the Gentiles. Those who had the benefit of the original invitation are perhaps best described by Paul in Romans 9:4-5—Jews with all their heritage and spiritual advantages."

It would have been shocking to first-century listeners that such a well-heeled host as God would think to call the poor and the blind and the lame (and the Gentiles!) to the banquet. It would have been better just to throw the food out! It was thought that because such people lacked bodily *wholeness* they also lacked proper *holiness*. As social *un*equals, they could never return the invitation (Lk. 14:13-14). They could never repay the host. But they still were called to the banquet!

No matter how we apply the story in its specific elements, we may agree that the sad observation of the parable, in verse 24, is shocking: "None of those who were invited will taste of my dinner." Yet the key point must not be lost: Those who are excluded from the banquet have only themselves to blame. And the same "servant"—Jesus—is right in our midst, too, summoning us all to a daily feast of relationship.

>> WISDOM FOR TODAY

Youth need to grapple with the issues of freedom and responsibility raised in this parable. We are free to choose whether or not to attend the "banquet" of God. Just as they are approaching the age of independence and freedom to do as they choose, they are also encountering more responsibility—confirmation, jobs, education, and relationships. The call to God's banquet always seems to come when we are busy preparing our own banquets. For the call speaks primarily to our freedom to either hold on to, or let go of, what we have planned for our own salvation.

Time to Eat... Come on In!

In Real Life — Exploring tough questions facing youth today

Kid-Age Memory

You're just a little kid, playing outside. You hear the call to come in and eat...

What are you doing?

What excuse do you give for being slow to respond—or not responding at all?

Current Reality

You're a busy teenager, faced with many opportunities and responsibilities. You also have lots of almost-adult freedom. You sense God calling you to pay more attention to spiritual matters...

What does the call to the "reign of God" sound like for you? (Describe any type of invitation that God may be extending to you these days. Try to be specific.)

What typical "play activity" lures your attention away from the source of the call?
(Draw a picture of the thing, person, or activity, and be ready to explain to others what it is.)

The Radical Reign : Session 2

Permission is granted to photocopy this handout for use with this session.

SESSION 3

THE SINNERS' CLUB >>>

>> KEY VERSE
"I tell you, there is joy in the presence of the angels of God over one sinner who repents." (Luke 15:10)

>> FAITH STORY
Luke 15:1-10 (The parables of the lost sheep and the lost coin)

>> FAITH FOCUS
When the Pharisees and teachers of the law criticized Jesus for eating with sinners, he told two short parables to show that God searches for us like a good shepherd would search for a lost sheep, or like a determined woman would search for a lost coin. The climax of both parables ushers us into the realm of heaven, where we encounter great rejoicing, because of God's wealth of acceptance and love for those society rejects. Our way of reckoning worthiness is not God's way. No lost person is unworthy of being found by God.

>> SESSION GOAL
Help participants dispel the notion that church is a club for "good" people, because God searches for all lost souls.

TEACHING PLAN

1. FOCUS 8-12 minutes
Ask: *What is the most valuable thing you brought with you to this meeting?* (It must be an object they actually have with them, such as money, wallet, watch, ring, shoe, or even a button.) Then instruct everyone to *close eyes*, and keep them closed. Tell them to *hide* the most valuable thing they brought with them, and say you'll give a prize to anyone who hides their "valuable" well enough to not get found. But they must keep eyes closed! (Allow for some chaos, as kids grope around to find a hiding place. Let them know that any open eyes warrant disqualification.)

Re-gather and say: *When I say "Go!" find one thing you think somebody hid and get it back to its owner. You'll have to ask lots of questions to find out what belongs to whom.*

When some owners have been found, award a small prize to people whose valuables remained hidden. Return all items to their owners, and move to Connect.

>> Materials needed and advance preparation

- Bibles
- Index cards, and small box or hat
- Pencils
- Wrap a penny—with a rubber band—in a piece of paper money, either a $5 or a $10 bill, and hide the wrapped-up penny somewhere not in the meeting room (even outside).
- Jar of 99 pennies
- Scene from the movie *Ferris Bueller's Day Off* (see Apply); player
- Small prize for best hiding (see Focus)

In Real Life | The Radical Reign 21

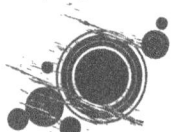

IS CHURCH...

- a way for people to "commit" a sin, go to confession or communion, get forgiven, and go out to sin all over again?

- a way to brainwash people into thinking if you "pray," everything good will happen to you?

- a place for people who can't think for themselves?

- where people with "wrong" beliefs are looked upon as subhuman?

2. CONNECT 5-7 minutes

Debrief by asking participants to share some of their real-life lost-and-found stories: *What is the most "valuable" thing you ever LOST or FOUND? Why did you look so hard for it?* After receiving some responses, move the discussion forward by saying: *Let's apply this idea of "valuable things" to <u>people</u> for a moment....*

- *Is there such a thing as "valuable" relationships? Explain.*
- *What about "valuable" people—who would they be?*
- *What is the danger of considering some people "valuable" to you?*

Shift to the next activity by saying: *For many people looking at the Christian church from the outside, the message of the gospel is that "good people will be saved." In Jesus' day, the "good" people were also the "valuable" people. But Jesus seemed to be forming more of a "sinners' club." ...*

3. EXPLORE THE BIBLE 12-15 minutes

Invite two people who enjoy reading to read aloud the parables in Luke 15:1-10. Then discuss:

- *Why would the "sinners" likely gather around Jesus? Who do you think those people were?*
- *Why were the Pharisees angry with Jesus?*
- *Why was eating with someone apparently such a big deal back then? Is it the same today?*
- *How would you describe the value of one sheep to a shepherd? One silver coin to a poor woman?* (Offer explanations here about shepherding and the dowry headband, as described in Insights from Scripture.)
- *How might the people who heard this parable have reacted to it? (the sinners? the Pharisees?) Why? How do you react to it?*

Note: In advance, you have wrapped a penny—using a rubber band—in a piece of paper money, either a $5 or a $10. Then you've hidden the wrapped-up penny somewhere outside the meeting room. You could even hide it outside.

Now hold up your jar of 99 pennies and say: *I only have 99 pennies in this jar, and one penny is missing; it's hidden somewhere in this building (or just outside). Would anyone here like to help me find it? Who would be willing to come back here every day this week, for at least 3 hours, to search until you find the penny?* Keep asking this "who would be willing" question, but keep lessening the search-requirement (for example: willing to come back tomorrow? Willing to spend 20 minutes looking right now? Willing to spend 5 minutes right now? etc.) until you have one person who is willing to do *at least something* to help you find the penny. (If you get more than one, either choose the person whose hand was raised first, or let more than one find the penny.) Say to that person: *Since you recognize that one penny's value, I'll tell you were to find it.*

Tell the person where to find the penny and let him or her enjoy the pleasant surprise of keeping the bill that is wrapped around it! Then discuss:

- *How was the value of this penny like, or unlike, the value of people in God's eyes?*
- *How was the joy of the person who found the penny like the joy of God upon "finding" a sinner who repents?*
- *How does the idea of grace come through to you in these parables?*
- *What do these parables tell you about the nature of God?*

4. APPLY 12-15 minutes

>> **Option A:** Play a very brief clip from the movie *Ferris Bueller's Day Off*. Use the scene in the principal's office when the secretary names all of the different groups in the school, using slang terms—dweebs, jocks, dorks, greasers, nerds, etc. Then move on to **"Activities for both options."**

>> **Option B:** If you don't use the movie clip, just name some of the ways kids were labeled in your own school when you grew up. Ask: *Do you still hear any of these names used to label people nowadays?* Move on to **"Activities for both options."**

Activities for both options: Next, distribute five index cards or slips of paper to each person. Pair up or form small groups to list categories of "outcasts" in their school—writing one name per index card or piece of paper. (Be clear they are to list categories of people, not individual names.) Tell them that the winner will be the team with the most entries at the end of 20 seconds.

When you call "TIME" and acknowledge the winner, ask the participants to sit in a circle and to call out the categories aloud. Then have everyone shuffle the cards and place them in a box or hat. Pass them around the circle, having each participant pick a card. Tell them that this is the type of person they'll have to eat lunch with at school every day for a solid week. Ask them to take a moment to imagine that and to think how they would feel about it. Then ask volunteers to share:

- *Would this be easy or hard for you to do? Why? How would you likely feel on day 1? Day 5?*
- *How would other friends likely respond to you, seeing you forming a relationship with this person?*
- *How would you feel about this person also being part of your "sinners' club" (your youth group or congregation)?*
- *Have you ever felt like an "outcast" yourself?* (Let participants know that they may "pass" or just answer yes or no.)

Wrap up by discussing: *In your opinion, how does this activity relate to what Jesus was saying in the parables of the lost sheep and the lost coin? Can you think of a different or more contemporary way to make the point?*

5. RESPOND 5-8 minutes

Here are two real-life situations. As you read each one aloud to the group, ask people to think about whether or not the person involved should be allowed into the "sinners' club" (the church). Should there be any rules about membership in the club?

1. Two girls, who have been very active in the youth group, have stopped coming to Sunday school and mass. After much questioning, you finally find out they've stopped coming because a male adult in the congregation has made some sexually suggestive comments to them on a number of occasions. The man, who has been attending for about two years, comes to mass about twice a month, but usually attends all social functions. At first the girls laughed at him, but now they don't want to come to church anymore if they think the man might be there.

Should be this man be allowed into the "sinners' club"? Should there be any rules about his membership in the club?

>>> **LOOK AHEAD**

For the next session you will need two large buckets and a short piece of hose. Practice siphoning water from one bucket to the other (see explanation of siphoning in Session 4).

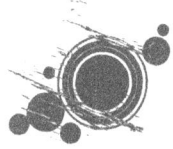

2. A person from the neighboring community has started coming to the church because of a health problem, hoping to get "right" with God. This person has no steady employment, but is willing to do odd jobs for people in the congregation. But some older people feel uncomfortable when the person shows up to work, especially when they are asked for advances on jobs not finished, or for loans. When people compare notes, it turns out that none of the borrowed money has been repaid in quite some time. Some church people feel the person is taking advantage of church connections with well-meaning people.

Should this person be allowed into the "sinners' club"? Should there be any rules about membership in the club?

Finally, ask: *Is there anyone connected with our parish who hasn't quite "made it" into our "sinners' club"? Why? What, if anything, do you think should be done?*

Close with a blessing: *May God find you wherever you are. May God give you the courage to welcome people into the "sinners' club," and to be welcomed by other sinners.*

 INSIGHTS FROM SCRIPTURE

One Bible scholar calls this section of Luke (chapters 15–19) the "Gospel of the Outcast." The compassion of Jesus for the social outcasts of that day comes through clearly. Of course, Jesus condemned sin in no uncertain terms, but unlike the religious leaders of his day, he showed that God offers the *remission* of sin, too. Thus the "sinners" congregated around him constantly.

›› A SHEEP AND A COIN: WHY BOTHER?

The Value of a Wayward Sheep. One hundred sheep would have been a common-sized herd in those days, though many were larger, being communal flocks. In such cases a large flock would belong to the whole village, with several shepherds watching over the sheep. A count of the sheep would have been done nightly when they came into the safety of a pen after a day of grazing in "open country."

The Value of a Single Coin. Some Bible students have suggested that the coin in the parable refers to one of the *drachmas* that made up a young woman's dowry, worn in the form of a headband. If so, we can understand the sentimental value of sweeping the hard earth floor until the coin would be found.

There were few windows in the houses of Palestine in those days, in many cases only a small, round opening, about two feet in diameter. If the earthen floor were covered with reeds, the sweeping could jostle the coin enough to make it tinkle or sparkle in the light of an oil lamp.

>> SINNERS: AVOID OR WELCOME THEM?

All three of the "lost" parables (sheep, coin, son) depend on introductory verses for their interpretation. They are the response to the Pharisees' criticizing Jesus because he "welcomed" sinners. The parables intend to justify the divine welcome of sinners.

Who were these outcasts? They were tax collectors and "sinners." The work of the *tax collector* was considered immoral, since it meant aiding an oppressive government against your own people. *Sinners* were people who failed to observe ritual purity laws (including ritual washing). Eating with them could mean spiritual contamination.

These two parables of the lost sheep and the lost coin would thus scandalize a Pharisee who was convinced that God's will required separation from the unclean. Surely the scriptures proclaimed avoidance of the sinner! How shocking, then, to hear a young rabbi preaching just the opposite—that God's basic attitude is to *welcome* people who are aware that they are sinners! Indeed, to hear Jesus tell it, these are the *only* people who can possibly be saved. Theologian Anders Nygren made the point that it is, indeed, only because we are lost that salvation is even possible (*Essence of Christianity*):

> "Humankind has always dreamed of fellowship with God on the basis of holiness. Christianity proclaims fellowship with God on the basis of sin. This is the meaning of (1) the gospel of Jesus: 'I came not to call the righteous, but sinners'; (2) Paul's doctrine of justification: It is the sinner whom God justifies..."

Thus the body of Christ (the church) is likewise called to welcome the outcast and the sinner. At its best, the church does not operate as a club for the righteous, but as a haven for sinners who desire fellowship with the One who found them.

>> 'FOUND' BEHAVIOR

Youth might ask whether they may behave any way they choose, knowing that God is like a loving shepherd or a determined woman who will search for them. God's searching love is set alongside the call to repent, the call to "prepare" for being found.

> "To compare God to a woman would shock and surprise the audience and challenge their fundamental image of God. The hearers are now challenged to see the searching woman as a metaphor for God's searching love, which paves the way for a new way of thinking about how God acts toward the sinner and the outcast."
>
> John R. Donahue, S.J., *The Gospel in Parable*

››› SESSION 4

STICK WITH ME! ››››

›› KEY VERSE

"I am the vine, you are the branches. Those who abide in me and I in them bear much fruit, because apart from me you can do nothing." (John 15:5)

›› FAITH STORY

John 15:1-7 (The vine and the branches)

›› FAITH FOCUS

The image of the vine and branches gives us yet another view of God—as the source and the sustainer of our being. *Why can't we go it alone, as society tells us we can?* Because without God we have no life and no meaning. Moreover, when we reach out and serve from the true vine's power, we bear fruit.

"Bearing fruit" is sometimes interpreted as works righteousness, but this is a foundational Bible passage. We bear fruit not in order to be grafted to the vine, but because we are *already* part of the vine.

›› SESSION GOAL

As teens face tough times of feeling alone, help them experience the comfort and confidence of knowing that they are connected to the Vine who sustains them.

›› Materials needed and advance preparation

- Two large buckets and a length of hose (for siphoning; see Focus)
- Potted plant (*optional*)
- Pencils
- Handout sheets for Session 4
- Bibles
- A length of clothesline (at least 30 ft. or 10 meters long), for Option A in Apply
- Props for Option B in Apply: Large pair of scissors, pruning shears or bottle of prune juice, piece of fruit, pillows or cushions

TEACHING PLAN

1. FOCUS 15-20 minutes minutes

››› **Option A:** Launch the session with an object lesson, teaching participants the valuable skill of siphoning. Bring in two large buckets and a length of hose. Let everybody take a turn trying it (see instructions on next page). Be ready for some messiness and fun! Talk about times when skillful siphoning is needed (e.g., on construction crews out in the wilderness, sometimes fuel must be transferred from one vehicle to another). Follow up by asking: *Why is it essential to keep the hose from pulling out of the water source, even for a second?*

>> **Option B:** Bring in a potted plant (or walk outside to find a plant or tree). Tell about what kind of plant it is and give some of its characteristics. Then ask: *If you had to give yourself a plant name that would describe your basic attitude toward life, what would it be? And why? For example, are you a:*

- **tiger lily?**
- **poison oak?**
- **weeping willow?**

Then ask this key question: *What is one thing that all plants have in common?* (If you have to, suggest this response: They must all be connected to something else—earth, water, sunlight, etc.—in order to grow.)

SIPHON

In a siphon, water flows up the inlet side of the hose, over the top of the pail, and down to the open end. Siphons work in a vacuum and do not depend on air pressure. The greater the height between the inlet and outlet, the faster the water will flow. A siphon stops when air gets into the hose and the intermolecular forces are broken.

Start the siphoning process by filling a bucket with water before placing it into its operating location, or by applying suction at the lower end after the piece of hose is in position. Once started, the flow will continue until the water level in both buckets is equal, or until air gets sucked in and stops the siphoning action.

2. CONNECT 5 minutes
Explain: *We've seen that "being connected," in some contexts, is absolutely crucial. Let's think about how that might be true for our personal spiritual growth, as well.*

- *When have you been "cut off" from a source of enjoyment, pleasure, or entertainment?* (like being grounded for punishment)
- *How does connectedness apply to your (or anyone's) relationship to God?*

Shift to the next activity by saying: *In our spiritual journeys we can be aware of being "connected" OR live as though we are "cut off" from our source of life. But what does it really mean to be <u>connected to Jesus</u>?*

3. EXPLORE THE BIBLE 12-15 minutes
Read John 15:1-7 aloud and give a very brief mini-lecture to explain the key elements of the parable. Be sure to cover these points:

- **The unity of believers**—the oneness—is experienced as all the branches are connected to a vine. They produce fruit: love, joy, peace, patience, kindness, goodness, faithfulness, gentleness, self-control (see Gal. 5:22, 23).
- **God, the Gardener, lovingly tends the vine.** God cares for it so that it will produce spiritual fruit (i.e., the spread of the gospel in the world and the influence of Christ's Spirit within individuals).
- **Pruning is always necessary with the vine.** Dead wood must be trimmed away so that the life and energy of the vine is channeled into fruit bearing, not for making foliage. That is, disciplines and trials produce strength and commitment in disciples. Loss is sometimes a key means of spiritual growth, especially when we "lose" whatever it is, apart from the Lord, that we believe is "saving" us.

Now distribute a copy of the handout sheet for Session 4 (along with a Bible) to each person. Give everyone enough time to mark some responses, drawing from the Bible passage. Follow up by asking volunteers to summarize their responses. Then spend a few minutes discussing the question at the bottom of the handout sheet: *How can our connection to Jesus help us make it through rough times? (Be practical!)*

4. APPLY 10 minutes

>> **Option A:** Stretch a length of clothesline rope from one end of the room to the other by tying each end to something solid. (Tie the rope between two trees if you can be outside.) Designate one end of the rope "at the end," and the other end "not close to the end." Say: *Think about the most awful day in your life so far. How close were you to the "end of your rope" on that day? (Was it a day of sadness, stress, grief, bad things happening, relationship breakup?) Stand by the rope at a place that demonstrates your response.*

Ask volunteers to share briefly about why they are standing where they are. Then have everyone take hold of the rope. Untie the ends of the rope and encircle everyone with it, while they're still holding on to their spot. (As you pull the rope around, everyone will be drawn closer in on each other.) Then, with everyone in a human "knot," offer this blessing: *This rope symbolizes our vine-connection to Jesus. He is the one who is with us through all things—our joys and sorrows—and gives us the strength to keep keeping on. Jesus has encircled us with his love and drawn us into close fellowship with our brothers and sisters, who can encourage and support us along the way.*

Continue with *Option A* under Respond, below.

>> **Option B:** Place the objects described below in different places in the room and then give these instructions: *Place yourself in the parable by choosing one of these statements as true of yourself* (write the statements below on chalkboard or newsprint). Have participants move to the place in the room near the object that is related to each statement. Then spend some time having volunteers explain why they chose a particular response:

- **Large pair of scissors:** I fear being "cut off" from God or others in situations like...
- **Pruning shears or a bottle of prune juice:** I need pruning because...
- **Piece of fruit:** I think I'm bearing some fruit because...
- **Some pillows, cushions, or blanket for sitting on:** I'd like to know what "abiding in him" really means when...

Continue with *Option B* under Respond, below.

5. RESPOND 3-5 minutes

>> **Option A:** As participants remain huddled together, wrap up by asking them to state what key struggle they experience in staying connected either to God or to friends, family, school, or church. Then, have everyone offer a silent prayer for fellow branches.

>> **Option B:** Discuss: *When we've been cut off, how can our connection to friends, family, school, or faith community supply us with what we need to go on?* If your group enjoys singing, sing together "I am the Vine and You are the Branches" by John Michael Talbot or "Vine and Branches" by Trevor Thomson. Sing either with piano or a cappella. Then close with this prayer or another prayer in your own words:

> Gardener God,
>   you have planted and protected us by your faithful hand.
> Our branches so intertwine with one another and with the Vine it is hard to know where
>   one ends and the other begins.
> May we learn to remain in You, that we may be sustained by the life that flows to us from
>   You through our fellow branches.
> Rooted in you, may we blossom and bear fruit for the life of the world. Amen.

>>> LOOK AHEAD

Bring a wooden baseball bat for Session 5. If you plan to use the Extender Session next, set a time to show the movie *A River Runs Through It.*

INSIGHTS FROM SCRIPTURE

This section of the Gospel of John is part of Jesus' so-called Farewell Discourse (encompassing 13:31 to 16:33), probably uttered either during the Passover meal or very soon after the institution of the Lord's Supper. It was Jesus' last chance, before his trial and crucifixion, to warn his disciples not to fall away from him.

The entire discourse included much interaction and dialogue between the disciples and Jesus, consisting of:

- **A.** Questions and answers (13:31–14:31)
- **B.** A speech about relationships (15:1-27)
- **C.** A discourse about revelation (16:1-33)

The parable of the vine and the branches is part of Jesus' speech about relationships; specifically, his relationship with the disciples. He would soon be leaving, and the relationship would change radically in nature: no more face-to-face teaching!

VINE CULTURE IN ANCIENT TIMES

Cultivating the grapevine was a common farming endeavor in ancient Palestine. One commentator, Merrill C. Tenney, says:

> "It is possible that if the text of this discourse was spoken as [Jesus and the disciples] walked from the upper room in Jerusalem down into the Kidron Valley and across to the Mount of Olives, they could have seen the great golden vine, the national emblem of Israel, on the front of the Temple."

The vine was so important to the Hebrews that ordinary citizens would donate their money to add another golden grape to the clusters on the Temple!

SUSTAINED BY THE TRUE VINE

What does it actually mean to be "sustained" by Jesus? It is to allow his life to permeate our thoughts and actions.

> "The branch does not come to the vine with its own agenda; it exists only to fulfill the purpose of the fruit-bearing vine. How often have we decided, without consulting God, what we wanted to do, then asked God to help us achieve it? That is not abiding. To abide, we must yield ourselves to God's purposes."
> —Marlene Kropf and Eddy Hall

Therefore, bearing fruit is not the first order of being part of the vine; *abiding* is. We bear fruit not in order to be grafted to the vine, but because we are *already* part of the vine.

> **Bearing fruit is not the first order of being part of the vine; abiding is. We bear fruit not in order to be grafted to the vine, but because we are already part of the vine.**

≫ SUSTAINING VINE

So many other things offer to carry us through life: the acceptance of friends, the ability to be successful and earn approval (through extracurricular activities at school, jobs, etc.), accomplishments, the pursuit of money and self-sufficiency. Though the Bible's comforting message is that Christ the Vine sustains us, we may nevertheless have to ask: How many youth even sense a need for God's sustaining presence? They may need help to recall the times of need in which they've come to *the end of their rope*. Nothing else could "save" them in a tough situation, accept faith in their Lord. Most adults have been there at some time. Many youth have not had that "opportunity" yet.

John 15:1-7
Cultivating Connection

Exploring tough questions facing youth today

The BENEFITS of staying connected and bearing fruit—

verse _____

verse _____

verse _____

verse _____

verse _____

The DANGERS of NOT staying connected and NOT bearing fruit—

verse _____

verse _____

verse _____

verse _____

verse _____

Discuss:
How can our connection to Jesus help us make it through rough times? (Be practical!)

The Radical Reign : Session 4

Permission is granted to photocopy this handout for use with this session.

>>> **SESSION 5**

AGAINST THE GRAIN >>>

>>> KEY VERSE

"...for all who exalt themselves will be humbled, but all who humble themselves will be exalted." (Luke 18:14b)

>>> FAITH STORY

Luke 18:9-14 (Parable of the Pharisee and the tax collector)

>>> FAITH FOCUS

This is one of several parables that teaches how to live in accordance with God's "upside-down" reign of God. By contrasting the Pharisee's attitude with that of a sinful, but humble, tax collector, Jesus showed that the true nature of salvation goes against the grain of accepted "works theology." Instead, God saves according to divine mercy rather than human merit. This parable highlights the "upside-down" nature of the gospel, the subversion of the usual order: the wealth of poverty, humility instead of pride, love of enemies, the power of powerlessness, and losing our lives to save them.

>>> SESSION GOAL

Encourage youth to "go against the grain" by being humble, even though their culture so loudly trumpets the value of personal pride.

>>> Materials needed and advance preparation

- Pencils
- Writing paper
- Bibles
- Copies of handout sheet for Session 5
- Wooden baseball bat
- Chalkboard/chalk or newsprint/markers
- A chair for each person (see Focus, Option A)

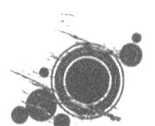 **TEACHING PLAN**

1. FOCUS 8-10 minutes

>>> **Option A:** Point out how tough it is to "go against the grain" (pull or push against each other) by playing one of the following games:

1. Set up chairs (one per person) in a circle, and assign a chair to each person (by color, a marker, a small personal item placed on it). Then have everyone make a tight huddle in the center of the circle by locking arms back-to-back. If you need to, spread out the chairs well enough so each person can get to one easily. Also spread out players who are physically strong.

On "GO," everyone starts tugging towards his or her chair without letting go of the rest of the group, *trying to tag their chair with a foot, knee, or hip* (you as leader decide which for each round). The first person to tag her chair gets to sit down. The object is to keep from being the last person to tag a chair. Once out, no one can move their chairs or those of other players. As the "huddle group" gets smaller, the game gets harder! (Game adapted from *Screamers & Scramblers*, by Michael W. Capps)

2. Play Red Rover, Red Rover. Your group may enjoy a chance to play again this children's game, where teams send representatives to break through the opposing team's line. This game is best played in a large area or outside.

Divide the group in half and form two lines facing each other, each at least 10 meters or 30 feet apart. Team members link hands tightly, then one team decides together who to "call over" from the other team. They chant together, "Red rover, red rover, let _____ come over." The person called pushes against and tries to break through the hand-locked line. If successful, the person chooses a player from that line and they return to the other team. If unsuccessful, the player joins the line that held. Continue until one line is down to one player.

Variation: Call more than one player over at a time. It will make it more difficult for the lines to hold.

>> **Option B:** For a less active opener, start with an acrostics activity. Define *humility* by having small groups work on acrostics of the word H-U-M-B-L-E on pieces of paper. Re-gather to decide on a whole-group acrostic by writing ideas on the chalkboard. Follow up with these questions:

- *How does the idea of being humble go against the grain of what our culture says it means be successful or "have it together"?*
- *Can you give any examples from your relationships in school or neighborhood?*

NORTH AMERICAN YOUTH SAY...

- you should be ready to "strut your stuff."
- chivalry is old-fashioned.
- a gracious winner is a wimp; a gracious loser is a fool.
- if I don't look out for myself, who will?
- "trash" talk (making yourself look good by picking on your opponent's faults) shows you're self-confident.

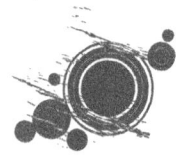

2. CONNECT 5-8 minutes

Ask:

- *When did you feel as though you, personally, were going against the grain or struggling against the rest of the crowd?*
- *Have you ever had to "go against the grain" because of your beliefs? Why? What happened?*

Shift to the next activity by saying: *Jesus' parables often went "against the grain" because they challenged conventional ideas. When he ran into people who thought they had their act together with God, Jesus gave them a whole new picture of what a righteous person was. It's called the parable of the Pharisee and the tax collector.*

3. EXPLORE THE BIBLE 7-15 minutes

Have volunteers read the actual words of the Pharisee and the tax collector in Luke 18:9-14.

Discuss: *What do you think God looks for when we pray?*

Then distribute copies of the handout sheet, "Practice Gratitude," and invite people to the gratitude or the "yes" practice described there.

Option: Keep the discussion open-ended, and wrap up by making this point: *Though acceptance with God comes by grace, we are still called to put ourselves in the place of receiving grace.* Then read the quote by Richard Foster (sidebar, next page). Discuss some or all of these questions: *In light of these words, what would you say about fasting and praying? Explain. What about the fasting and praying of the Pharisee/tax collector? Do you think regular fasting and praying makes one more humble before God?*

You might invite your group to practice praying or fasting as a spiritual discipline. Examples: Set a schedule for regular Bible reading, or a set amount of time for daily prayer, or a specific length of time for some type of fast (from food, movies, music, etc.).

Stress that God's grace frees us up to do disciplined things out of gratitude rather than out of fear or trying to impress someone. Anything we accomplish in life takes discipline. This is true in God's radical reign as well. But we have the motive of love and the power of the indwelling Spirit to help us.

4. APPLY 15-20 minutes

Now direct everyone's attention to the last sentence of verse 14. Say: *On TV, in the movies, or in the news the rich, powerful, confident, and dominant people are heroes. But the teachings of Jesus go against the grain and turn these values upside down. Jesus stressed things like the wealth of poverty, being humble instead of being proud, loving enemies instead of beating them to a pulp, the power that can come from being powerless, and losing our lives in order to save them. Can you imagine how the media would have to change, if it were to begin showing these against-the-grain attitudes?*

Hand out paper and pencils for jotting notes and ask participants to work as individuals, pairs, or small groups to choose a TV show, a movie, or even the news. The task is to rewrite the basic plot—or a particular scene—of the show or film, with Jesus' against-the-grain values as a replacement. For example, Rambo VII might show a hero who walks away from a name-caller, rather than slashing off his head! Here are some other cultural "DO's" to get your group thinking about what shows they might rewrite:

- *get revenge or "payback"*
- *take no "baloney" from anybody*
- *in sports: hotdogging, dancing after a touchdown, or "trash-talking" other players*
- *products for the "in crowd" or "cool" people*
- *ads that put down "nerdy" people*
- *being #1, or being the winner and looking down on "losers"*
- *being rich*
- *being powerful*
- *being in style*
- *TV shows and movies that glorify power*

> "A farmer is helpless to grow grain; all he can do is to provide the right conditions for the growing of grain. He puts the seed in the ground where the natural forces take over and up comes the grain. That is the way with the spiritual disciplines—they are a way of sowing to the Spirit. The disciplines are God's way of getting us into the ground; they put us where [God] can work within us and transform us."

Richard Foster,
Celebration of Discipline

LOOK AHEAD

For next session, contact two group members (or adults) to fake a fight (Focus).

5. **RESPOND** 8-10 minutes

Hold up the wooden baseball bat. Ask a baseball player in the group (or a fan of the game) to explain about how to hold a wooden baseball bat with the label up. That way, the bat won't shatter as it might when hitting the ball "against the grain."

Have everyone sit in a circle and tell them you are going to pass the baseball bat to each person, in turn, until it travels around the circle. When the bat comes around, they fill in the blank at the end of this sentence. Write it on the chalkboard or newsprint:

"In my life right now, I could go 'against the grain' a little more by _____."

Explain that "going against the grain" might mean different things to different people in the group. So each person should explain what he or she means. Here are some examples of possible responses:

- *I will speak up more for justice, even if it causes some problems.*
- *I will call a thing wrong, if it really is.*
- *I will respect my parents' values and traditions more.*
- *I will face up to violence and conflict.*
- *I will listen with patience and acceptance.*
- *I will be willing to lose, to be made fun of, or just be uncool in order not to compromise my values.*
- *I will learn more about what it means to be humble before God.*

Leave the interpretation wide open; just ask participants to explain what they mean, personally—i.e., how they feel they could perhaps push to the edge of their comfort zone in order to respond to the parable as they've understood it.

Put the bat in the middle of the circle, and close by praying that God will help each person follow through on their self-challenge.

 # INSIGHTS FROM SCRIPTURE

Jesus never claimed that entering the reign of God would be easy. The parable of the Pharisee and the tax collector, and the two following sayings (vv. 15-17 and 18-30), upend our notions of what it takes to "get there." All three stories stress the inability of people to *earn* God's approval.

A SHOCKING STORY

The Pharisee followed the accepted custom in his society:

1. *going* to the temple in order to pray;
2. *standing* to pray, likely speaking the words aloud; and
3. *separating* from those considered less holy.

In regard to the last point, Walter Liefeld comments (in the *Expositor's Bible Commentary*): "This [separating] was not in itself reprehensible, because at the inception of Pharisaism there was a need for a distinctive group who would maintain a piety that stood in contrast to the encroaching pagan Hellenism [Greek culture]." Yet this man in the parable had clearly gone too far, basing the separation on the supposed merits of his own works.

It may be difficult for us to feel the impact that the story would have had on the original hearers. One reason for this is that we already tend to view the Pharisees, through years of conditioning in Sunday school, as opposed to Jesus. But just the opposite sentiment would have prevailed in the first century!

The Pharisee would have been seen as living a truly laudable life, sincerely fulfilling the will of God in a way that the average citizens failed to do. He would normally have deserved high praise from any young rabbi like Jesus. And the tax collector, a political and religious failure, would have deserved at the least a righteous tongue-thrashing. Would it help us to substitute modern-day equivalents? How about using a respected church leader for the Pharisee's part, and a spy caught selling government secrets? Who's shocked then?

A CALL TO HUMILITY

A key point of the parable is to show us the place of true humility before God. People of all cultures and eras make heroes of those who are anything but humble. By contrasting the Pharisee's arrogant attitude with that of a sinful, but humble, tax collector, Jesus showed that the true nature of salvation goes against the grain of the standard, accepted "works theology." Instead, God saves according to divine mercy rather than human merit.

Bible commentator R. C. H. Lenski makes the point that the Greek verb translated "merciful" is actually the word most commonly translated "expiation," or "making amends." Thus, it might be better to translate, "Make amends in regard to me." This slant on the tax collector's plea suggests that he was asking God to make a sacrifice for his atonement. According to Jewish custom, it would have been appropriate to "make amends" by making a sacrifice. That is exactly what God did. Jesus became the sacrificial lamb, the one to "make amends" for sinners—and tax collectors.

 "What good is prayer? Not much, if by our prayers we insist on imposing our will on the world, on life. But if we can repent of that folly, if we can pray as the Spirit helps us to pray, 'Not my will, but yours, O God, be done,' then prayer can be the greatest good, a blessed gift from the Holy Giver."

Ken Gibble,
www.kenslines.blogspot.com

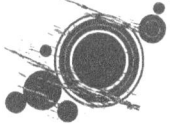

Practice gratitude

In Real Life — Exploring tough questions facing youth today

End your day with this practice. Another way is to pause periodically in your day and notice something good within your sight or hearing, and say "yes" to it. "Yes" to that spreading tree, "Yes" to that flying ball, "Yes" to the warm blanket, "Yes" to the raspberry. As you do this, notice what happens inside you.

"If the only prayer you would say in your whole life is 'thank you,' that would suffice." (Meister Eckhart, 13th-century Christian mystic)

"The great thing is prayer. Prayer itself. If you want a life of prayer, the way to get it is by praying.... You start where you are and you deepen what you already have."

(Thomas Merton, 20th-century monk, writer, and social activist)

"What good is prayer? Not much, if by our prayers we insist on imposing our will on the world, on life. But if we can repent of that folly, if we can pray as the Spirit helps us to pray, 'Not my will, but yours, O God, be done,' then prayer can be the greatest good, a blessed gift from the Holy Giver."

(Ken Gibble, www.kenslines.blogspot.com)

The Radical Reign : Session 5

Permission is granted to photocopy this handout for use with this session.

SESSION 6

LOVE IS AN ACTION WORD!

KEY VERSES

"Which of these three, do you think, was a neighbor to the man who fell into the hands of the robbers?" [The expert in the law] said, "The one who showed him mercy." Jesus said to him, "Go and do likewise." (Luke 10:36-37)

FAITH STORY

Luke 10:25-37 (Parable of the Good Samaritan)

FAITH FOCUS

When the expert in the law asked who his neighbor was, he was looking for a way to make sure that he was righteous. Jesus made it harder on him than expected! It would not be a simple matter of picking out the people towards whom he should show kindness. Rather, Jesus said he must be ready to show compassion to whoever needs help. He must also be ready to receive mercy at the hands of the least lovable one who offers it.

SESSION GOAL

Though participants would most often rather eliminate their enemies, help them consider ways to show active compassion, seeking to turn enemies into friends.

Materials needed and advance preparation

- Construction paper
- Scissors
- Pencils
- Bibles
- Copies of handout sheets for Session 6
- Contact two students (or adults) to fake a fight.
- Props for volunteer actors to use during Scripture reading (see Explore): small pillows, a large shirt, a broom or stick horse, box of adhesive bandages, watering can, two silver coins.
- Index cards

TEACHING PLAN

1. FOCUS 8-10 minutes

Option A: In advance, arrange for a fake "bully" to haul a teen (boy) out of the meeting area. From the other room (or closet) come the exaggerated sound effects of a fight: *Ouch! Oh! Whack!* (But participants will know it's all fake, hokey, and funny.) Then the group member—not the bully—comes back in and reports: "I think he's in pretty bad shape."

Say: *Imagine an enemy really had attacked one of our group members and had been hurt like this.*
You have only enough cell battery power to make one call, either to an AMBULANCE company or to the POLICE station (there is no 911 service in your area). Which would you choose? Why?

In Real Life | The Radical Reign 39

When everyone has made a choice, spend some time discussing what it means, in practical terms, *to choose to treat an enemy with compassion.*

>>> **Option B:** Tell participants that you are going to read a series of potentially controversial statements. After reading each one, ask people to move toward one end of the room if they AGREE with the statement, and towards the other end if they DISAGREE with the statement. As each statement is read and people move to their positions, ask volunteers to explain their responses. (Don't try to come to any firm conclusions; you are just getting people thinking about the topic.) Follow up with the discussion questions in Connect.

Agree or Disagree?

- If an ex-convict had a flat tire, you should stop and help him fix it.
- I warned some hikers to take along plenty of water. They forgot the canteen and got sunstroke. I'd be the first to volunteer to take them to the hospital.
- If a Satanist offered to take care of me while I was very sick, I'd accept the help.
- It's better to go ahead and help someone, even if you have a bad attitude about it.

MANY YOUTH...

- may define enemies as those who violate a supreme value for them: the principle of "fairness."

- tend to look for the potential of reciprocal action when considering "putting out" for someone, relying on the principle of "you scratch my back, and I'll scratch yours."

- want to know the "payoff" in any call to commitment, sacrifice, or difficult challenge.

2. CONNECT 5-7 minutes

Give each person three index cards. Give these instructions: *On each card, jot one thing that you either <u>need</u> or <u>don't need</u> help doing in your life.* (Let participants know how you'll be using the cards after they respond.)

Gather the cards, shuffle them, and read them aloud. Ask participants to match items on the cards with group members who wrote them. Ask them to share WHY they need or don't need help with each item.

Ask the group to summarize their understanding of the Bible's teaching about "helping others." How would they say it in one sentence so even a first-grader could understand?

Shift to the next activity by saying: *Helping usually sounds like a good thing, but there can be complications. Jesus told a parable about helping that was full of potential complications. Let's find out what his point was....*

3. EXPLORE THE BIBLE 10-12 minutes

Distribute the first handout sheet, and go over the instructions there. Place these props on a table, ready for volunteer actors to use: small pillows (for beating the victim); a large shirt (clothes to be stripped); a broom or stick horse (for a "horse" to ride); a box of adhesive bandages (for bandaging the victim); a watering can (for "pouring" oil); and two silver coins.

Choose your volunteer actors, and emphasize that as all group members read through the passage in unison, they must stop at the bold parts in order for actors to take up the props and do the action. Assign a lead reader who will stop and begin the readings; participants will join in on cue. (**Note:** The last bold part is left open-ended. What will your actors do when they come to the words, "Go and do likewise"?)

After the acted-out reading, discuss:

- *Why did Jesus tell this story? What point was he trying to make?*
- *What does "Go and do likewise" actually mean? Do you agree with what the "actors" did when they came to that part? Would you have done something else?*
- *Be the law expert. How well has Jesus answered your questions (in vv. 25 and 29)? What would be your attitude after hearing this parable?*

4. APPLY 15-20 minutes

Option A: (for groups of more than 6):

Ask everyone to sit in a circle and close their eyes. Tell participants to keep their eyes closed and to exchange places with the person whom they think is sitting directly opposite them in the circle (still keeping eyes closed). Then say:

The question that the law expert asked was: "Who is my neighbor?" So...still keeping your eyes closed, shake hands with the person on your right and on your left. Make a guess about who your neighbors are—<u>without talking or making any other sound.</u>

Have people open their eyes and tell whether they guessed their neighbors' identities correctly. Brainstorm for a few minutes about: *Who are our "neighbors" today—in the biblical sense that Jesus was talking about?* Make the point that neighbors are those we find on our right and our left, wherever we are. Remind the group to take note, next time they are in a crowd of strangers, of the people on their right and left. They may be surprised to find who their neighbors are! Say: *Let's put ourselves in this story to discover the ways it would apply to us today.*

On chalkboard or newsprint, work together to develop a <u>Top Five List of Teens' Knock-out Hurts Today</u>. Jot suggestions as they are called out. Stress that these should be teen problems today that tend to **knock teens out and leave them bleeding alongside the road** (at least metaphorically!). Youth might suggest, for example: having fights with parents; facing betrayal by friends; being tempted to drink alcohol or have premarital sex; not making grades; finding enough free time for school, work, friends, sports; not having a safe place to sleep at night.

When you've narrowed your list to the top five items, go back to each one and ask: *Do you know someone who struggles with this? In what ways could you come to such a person's aid? In what ways might a teen receive help from unlikely sources?*

Keep the brainstorming and problem solving as practical as possible. Let participants know they should feel free to admit their own struggles in any of the areas, but that they are not required to do so. The point is to explore real forms of help for real problems.

Option B: If your group is smaller than six people, give a brief mini-lecture on the concept of "tough love." Make the point that helping someone sometimes requires being firm in setting boundaries and limits on the relationship. Give an example of a time when you, personally, have chosen NOT to do the most immediately pain-reducing (or symptom-relieving) thing for a person, in favor of a compassion that seeks a more long-range, lasting change in the person or circumstances. Invite participants to tell their own stories about this, either as givers or receivers of tough love. Your discussion might focus around this basic question:

> **When a person is hungry, is it better to give them a fish—or show them how to use a hook, line, and pole?**

Ask: *Which would you like someone to give you?*

5. RESPOND 10-12 minutes

Distribute the second handout sheet, "Enemies into Friends." Ask each person to sketch a picture of a person they know whom they might consider an enemy. (Let them know that they won't have to reveal who this is.) On one side write the word: ENEMIES.

First, challenge them (in pairs or small groups) to play a word game that many of them may be familiar with. Turn ENEMIES into FRIENDS in the fewest number of steps possible. The rules are:

1. *Each step requires writing down seven letters.*
2. *To arrange any number of letters in a different order requires one step.*
3. *To substitute one letter for another requires one step. For example, to change FEAR to LOVE would require 4 steps, as follows:*

FEAR	Answer: ENEMIES
1. ARFE	1. EEIENMS
2. LRFE	2. FEIENMS
3. LOFE	3. FRIENMS
4. LOVE	4. FRIENDS

Declare a winning pair or team and then ask your key response question: *What four steps could you take to try to turn your real-life enemies into friends (neighbors)?*

Pray for the ability to make this change in real life.

INSIGHTS FROM SCRIPTURE

The parable of the Good Samaritan was Jesus' response to two questions (in vv. 25 and 29) posed by an "expert in the law." To be such an expert meant to be thoroughly versed in the details and requirements of the Jewish religion, in this case the well-worn question as to who one's neighbor might be. This question was important to the scribes because it was a key element in the interpretation and application of the commandment stated in verse 27.

>> DANGEROUS JOURNEY, FOOLISH TRAVELER

The journey from Jerusalem to Jericho was 17 miles of downhill, curving, pitted paths, filled with rocks and places for thieves to hide out. The journey was treacherous and ordinary citizens avoided it unless they traveled in sufficient numbers. Hearers of the story would have been familiar with the reputation of the road. It had been dubbed, after all, "The Bloody Way."

The parable's traveler would have been considered foolish by the ordinary hearer of Jesus' day. So...do we help even those who have no one to blame for their problems except themselves? The parable, in effect, asks us to consider: Is this not what God has done for us?

>> ONE MAN STOPS TO HELP

Priests served in the temple at Jerusalem, carrying out their duty to offer sacrifices for atonement. The Levites normally served in other capacities in the temple, related to the holding of services and maintenance chores. Both the priest and Levite in the story passed by the wounded traveler.

Some scholars have suggested that the two clerics avoided the man, thinking that he was dead; they would have been concerned about violating the legal prohibition about touching a dead body. Others have suggested that people were well aware that robbers would use apparently wounded decoys in order to lure people into stopping along the way. It's a common concern today, too. However, the point of Jesus' story seems to beg the question of whether these were good enough reasons to pass by the wounded traveler.

A neighbor was typically considered to be a fellow Jew—certainly not a Samaritan. The hate-history between the two groups began after the 722 BC exile of Northern Kingdom Jews to Assyria. The subsequent deportations and infiltrations brought intermarriages between the Gentiles and Jews that were considered impure. Jews of Jesus' time would have been infuriated by these half-pagan Samaritans who claimed cherished patriarchs like Abraham and Moses as their ancestors. Racially and religiously, then, the Samaritans were the untouchables of the community.

Upon mention of the Samaritan in Jesus' story, the listeners would have assumed that the villain had arrived! Yet only the Samaritan stopped to help. Jesus showed the merciful man not only taking pity—which is a feeling—but translating that feeling into sacrificial action. How self-sacrificing is the act shown to be? In real life, it would have meant using pieces of his own clothing for bandages, using his own wine as a medicine, paying out of his own funds for further care, and putting himself in future debt to the innkeeper. There is no mention of an agreement that the wounded traveler would later repay him. Love is an action word, with the consequences of loving action being potentially painful.

>> LET AN ENEMY HELP?

Parables call for personal decision; thus Jesus' concluding question in verse 36. This parable ends with, "Go and do likewise." Be good to those in pain, but also go and allow the "enemy" to serve you. This is the angle of the parable that is often overlooked. The Jew who is beaten is helped only by his enemy. This parable is as much about allowing love from unexpected and unlikely sources as it is about helping the afflicted.

The Word in Action
Luke 10:25-37 (NRSV)

INSTRUCTIONS: Follow your Lead Reader as you read this passage in unison with the other group members. **STOP** for the action after each of the bold-faced words or phrases.

25 Just then a lawyer **STOOD UP** to test Jesus. "Teacher," he said, "what must I do to inherit eternal life?"

26 He said to him, "What is written in the law? What do you read there?"

27 He answered: "You shall love the Lord your God with all your heart, and with all your soul, and with all your strength, and with all your mind; and your neighbor as yourself."

28 And he said to him, "You have given the correct answer; do this, and you will live."

29 But wanting to justify himself, he asked Jesus, "And who is my neighbor?"

30 Jesus replied, "A man was going down from Jerusalem to Jericho, and **FELL** into the hands of robbers, who **STRIPPED HIM**, **BEAT HIM**, and went away, leaving him half dead.

31 Now by chance a priest was **GOING DOWN THAT ROAD**; and when **HE SAW** him, he **PASSED BY** on the other side.

32 So likewise a Levite, when he **CAME TO THE PLACE** and saw him, **PASSED BY** on the other side.

33 But a Samaritan while **TRAVELING** came near him, and when he saw him, he **WAS MOVED WITH PITY**.

34 He went to him and **BANDAGED** his wounds, having **POURED OIL AND WINE** on them. Then he put him on his own animal, brought him to an inn and **TOOK CARE** of him.

35 The next day he **TOOK OUT TWO DENARII [SILVER COINS], GAVE THEM** to the innkeeper, and said, 'Take care of him; when I come back, I will repay you whatever more you spend.'

36 Which of these three, do you think, was a neighbor to the man who fell into the hands of the robbers?"

37 He said, "The one who showed him mercy." Jesus said to him, "**GO AND DO LIKEWISE.**"

The Radical Reign : Session 6

Permission is granted to photocopy this handout for use with this session.

ENEMIES into FRIENDS

Exploring tough questions facing youth today

Fill the back of this sheet with a sketch of a person you consider an enemy. (You don't have to reveal who it is). Inside this sketch write the word: ENEMIES.

Next, turn ENEMIES into FRIENDS in the fewest number of steps possible.

Rules:
1. Each step requires writing down seven letters.
2. To arrange any number of letters in a different order uses up one step.
3. To substitute one letter for another uses up one step.

Example: FEAR to LOVE
1. ARFE
2. LRFE
3. LOFE
4. LOVE

The Radical Reign : Session 6

"It's easy to ignore violence, conflict, and 'others.' I could separate myself entirely from almost any hard situation, caring only about myself…. But if just one person could start caring about others and actually listen to them, might the barriers between 'friends' and 'others' start to crumble? Could the barriers between different groups weaken to the point where violence isn't necessary to command respect from others? Could genuine respect for others start to grow?"

Gabriella Stocksdale, 15, Elgin, IL

Permission is granted to photocopy this handout for use with this session.

>>> **EXTENDER SESSION**

THE GOOD SHEPHERD (JOHN 10:1-18)

>> SESSION GOAL

Help participants accept, freely and responsibly, the outreaching love of the Good Shepherd who seeks us.

Use this parable to expand on the parable of the vine and branches. As branches, we receive sustaining life from the true vine. This is possible only because God has first offered the ultimate sacrifice to save us. But our part is crucial: to accept the love and help we need. We do have the choice to turn away from that love, with devastating consequences.

>> SUGGESTED ACTIVITY

Announce a movie night and show *A River Runs Through It* (PG, 124 minutes). The film highlights the difference it makes in a young person's life when he is able—or unable—to receive offered love. The film shows how two boys respond to their father's shepherding love and guidance . . . and go separate ways.

>> POSSIBLE DISCUSSION THEMES AND QUESTIONS

Two young men seem to compete for their father's attention and admiration, but in different ways: Norman by being a "good boy," Paul by being a "bad boy." Both need to see the look of pride in their father's eyes. In a key scene, Norman and Paul are at the river bank, talking in the bright sunlight about a needy acquaintance.

> Paul: I thought we were supposed to help him.
> Norman: How do you help [him]?
> Paul: By taking him fishing.
> Norman: He doesn't like fishing.
> Paul: Well, maybe what he likes is somebody *trying* to help him.

Norman is struck by Paul's statement, and there is a long silence. It's obvious that Paul is also speaking of himself, as he looks up to the sky.

- *How would you describe what must happen inside a person—the "giving in" that must take place—in order to receive love from God and others? When have you had to give in, or give up your pride, in that way? Describe how holding on to pride can be a form of holding on to personal pain—as Paul seemed to do.*

- *Why does Paul, in effect, eventually reject his father's and brother's love? If his self-destructive actions were actually a cry for help, why couldn't he receive the help that his family held out to him?*

- *When you see another person "acting out," are you more likely to push him or her away or come closer, seeking to help?*

- *How would you respond to someone who says: "We need to clean up our act before God can love us"? Relate your response to Romans 5:8-10.*

Exploring tough questions facing youth today

CLUELESS AND CALLED
Discipleship and the Gospel of Mark

What does it take to be a disciple? This study of the Gospel of Mark focuses on the requirements for following Jesus' way and the abundant life that is ours as a result. (5 sessions)

DO MIRACLES HAPPEN?
Signs and Wonders in the Gospel of John

The greatest miracle, recorded in John 1:14 and 3:16, is the miracle of God's love that became flesh and lived among us. But John also included examples of what we more traditionally think of as miracles: the wonder of abundance from little; healing; signs of impossibility and faith; and the resurrection. (5 sessions)

DO THE RIGHT THING
Ethics Shaped by Faith

How do you know what's right and what's wrong? Even when you figure it out, the right thing is often the unpopular or unpleasant choice. This unit offers participants a clearer sense of what it means to claim a faith identity, a foundation that can help them sort out the gritty details of ethics shaped by faith. (6 sessions)

FIGHT RIGHT
A Christian Approach to Conflict Resolution

This unit will help youth understand conflict and its function. They will learn how they can be honest and loving, and explore how conflict can be used for positive results. They will also learn ways to enhance their communication skills. 1 Corinthians. (5 sessions)

GOD IS A WARRIOR?
Violence in the Bible

The Bible challenges us to be reconciled to one another and work for justice. So what do we do with the stories that seem to condone violence or even encourage it? A discussion of issues in the Old and New Testaments. (6 sessions)

HOW DO YOU KNOW?
Wisdom in the Bible

Wisdom literature teaches us that we gain knowledge of the world, ourselves, and God through experience and observation. This unit provides practical, hands-on wisdom to help young people avoid life's snares and grow closer to God. Proverbs, Job, Ecclesiastes. (5 sessions)

HOW TO BE A TRUE FRIEND
The Bible Reveals Friendship's Heart

To be a friend takes skill. Help youth discover the secrets of friendship through various stories from the Old and New Testament. (6 sessions)

HOW TO READ THE BIBLE
Building Skills for Bible Study

What kind of book is the Bible? What does this book mean to me? This unit looks at the Bible as revelation, as history, as literature. Selected scripture. (5 sessions)

KEEPING THE GARDEN
A Faith Response to God's Creation

If Christians believe that God made the world, we do not need any more compelling reason to care for it than that God has handed us a treasure to hold and protect. This unit gets beyond trendy environmentalism and challenges youth to see environmental awareness as a religious issue. Genesis. (6 sessions)

MANTRAS, MENORAHS, AND MINARETS
Encountering Other Faiths

How is Christianity different from other faiths? Why do others believe the way they do? This study can give youth a new appreciation for the uniqueness of Jesus. Selected scripture. (5 sessions)

SALT, LIGHT, AND THE GOOD LIFE
The Beatitudes and the Sermon on the Mount

What can youth expect in a life of discipleship? This unit explores the Sermon on the Mount under four main sections: the Beatitudes, Salt and Light, Jesus and the Law, and Heavenly Teachings. Matthew 5. (6 sessions)

A SPECK IN THE UNIVERSE
The Bible on Self-Esteem and Peer Pressure

Discover God's unconditional love and acceptance of all people. This study will show positive ways to have one's life make a difference, and help youth find ways to resist negative peer pressure and turn it into positive action. (6 sessions)

THE RADICAL REIGN
Parables of Jesus

Jesus used parables to reveal what the kingdom of God is like, and how God relates to us. This study highlights how the parables reveal God's reign as radically different from the world we live in, and what that means for the Christian life. (6 sessions)

TESTING THE WATERS
Basic Tenets of Faith

Discover the biblical roots for the central Christian concepts of covenant, community, and baptism. This short course is a way to test the (baptismal) waters of Christianity before diving in, or review the basics for those who already have. (6 sessions)

WHO IS GOD?
Engaging the Mystery

God is beyond human comprehension, yet desires to be known. These sessions focus on the way we get clues about and glimpses of God from the Bible, God's creation, and church tradition. Selected scripture. (5 sessions)

www.ingramcontent.com/pod-product-compliance
Lightning Source LLC
Chambersburg PA
CBHW080408170426
43193CB00016B/2854